LEN[illegible] DEVOTIONS
STATIONS *and* MEDITATIONS *from the* ROSARY SHRINE

Lawrence Lew, O.P.

All booklets are published thanks to the generosity of the supporters of the Catholic Truth Society

Nihil Obstat
P. Richardus Finn, O.P., DPhil
Censor deputatus

Imprimi potest
R.P. Martinus Ganeri, O.P., M.A., MPhil, DPhil
Prior Provincialis
Die 22nd Novembris MMXXII

The bible quotations in this booklet are from the Revised Standard Version of the Bible.

ISBN 978 1 78469 753 2

Contents

About this Book

This book presents three distinct Lenten devotions that are part of the life of St Dominic's Priory Church, the Rosary Shrine, in London: the Stations of the Cross, prayed on Fridays in Lent; the Canticle of the Passion, also prayed on Fridays in Lent; and the meditations on the Seven Last Words of Our Lord, which are preached in Holy Week.

The paintings of the Stations of the Cross presented here are in the Rosary Shrine Church, and they were painted by Nathaniel Westlake in 1887; his signature appears at the bottom of the fourteenth station. Westlake is renowned as a stained-glass designer, but he also painted some very notable works for churches, including the ceiling for St Joseph's in Highgate, and the monumental Stations of the Cross in the College Chapel of St Patrick's College, Maynooth, Ireland, which are based on these in St Dominic's, London. The London stations were canonically erected on 9th March 1887.

In this book, the titles that accompany each station are translated from the Latin inscriptions on the walls of St Mary's Seminary Chapel in Houston, Texas.

The Canticle of the Passion is a compilation of the words of Christ, drawn largely from Scripture, but arranged thus in a private revelation to the Dominican nun St Catherine de Ricci who lived in Florence in the sixteenth

century. For a twelve-year period, once a week, she would mystically share in Christ's passion and receive the sacred stigmata from noon on Thursday to four o'clock on Friday afternoon. It was shortly after this experience of the Lord's passion began that St Catherine composed her Canticle, which many Dominican nuns pray every Friday in Lent.

Finally, the Seven Last Words of Our Lord have, from the sixteenth century, been the subject of meditations on Good Friday. The set of reflections presented here was first preached in Holy Week of 2022, during the Rosary Shrine's annual "Holy Week Retreat".

STATIONS of the CROSS

Introduction

The most extraordinary path ever travelled, which was foreseen from all eternity by the God of love, was the route that Jesus walked from Gabbatha to Golgotha, from the pavement of Pilate's judgement hall to the place of the skull or Calvary where the God-Man mounted his judgement seat of the cross. Each step Christ took was motivated by his infinite love for humanity, and each drop of blood he shed along the way would have been, in itself, sufficient to heal man of the wounds of sin and bridge the chasm that, because of sin, exists between God and man. Yet, Christ shed his blood copiously along this way, so that it was encrimsoned like some royal route, and so that it became, in fact, the *via amoris*, the way of God's undying love.

And as with all of God's dealings with us, he works extraordinary feats, things beyond the ken or limits of our human nature, but hidden beneath aspects that, were it not revealed to us, we would once have deemed most ordinary and even profane, prosaic, and certainly unworthy of the divine. We see this in the matter of the sacraments, in the often-inadequate forms that we try to give to the sacred Liturgy, and indeed, in each human person who is transformed by grace to become a dwelling for the Holy Trinity. All this is because, in God's great love, his journey took the eternal *Logos* from heaven's heights to become flesh and dwell among us.

The way of the cross, which took Jesus through the streets of Jerusalem, is still today a very human and ordinary way – the route winds its way through quite mundane and undistinguished alleys and roads in a busy and sometimes chaotic urban environment. In a city as ancient as Jerusalem, one feels the weight of humanity and history; here is a place that feels lived in and worn down by all the momentous human triumphs and tragedies it has witnessed. A mass of humanity, a din of various languages, and the jostling of peoples, cultures and historical tensions continue to fill the streets as people throng the narrow passages and pious pilgrims attempt to make their way through the mass of city-folk trying to get on with their business and livelihoods. One feels along the streets that we call the *via crucis* or *via dolorosa* the closeness of the sorrows of our humanity, and the daily crosses of our human toil, as people pass you by, forgetful or even ignorant of the cosmic-changing significance of that walk once taken by Jesus Christ along this way, carrying the cruciform burden of our humanity on his shoulders. Here God passed along our way, and we passed him by. And this still happens in the present.

But the streets also thrum with life and activity, with shopkeepers hawking their wares, children calling out and playing, women laden down with bags or catching up on news over coffee, men gambling or arguing in groups, clustered around televisions as they discuss the rough and tumble of football or Middle Eastern politics. All life unfolds and unravels along the *via crucis*.

In this way, God wills to show us the depths of his love – by traversing our roads, entering our lives, coming close to our wounded humanity in all its complexities and pains. The way of the cross thus goes through our bedrooms, our offices, our cities, our neighbourhood cafés and corner shops, our schools and factories, and even through our friendships and marriages and relationships, and right into our hearts. For Heart speaks to heart, and the Lord's journey to the cross is impressed upon our world and our ways so that Christ can speak to us today. More in his actions than in words, Christ the Word Incarnate speaks of God's way for us, which is love.

Through these images of the way of the cross, and through these meditations on Christ's passion and his love for you and me, my hope is that you will be impressed – in every sense of the word – by the weight and madness and intensity of God's love for us, that you will be renewed in your baptismal commitment to follow that way of love, and that, having followed Christ to the end, you and I will also share in Love's victory over sin, death and all the woes of our mortal nature.

Note: "A plenary indulgence is granted to the faithful who make the pious exercise of the Way of the Cross. Those who are impeded can gain the same indulgence if they spend at least one half-hour in pious reading and meditation on the passion and death of our Lord Jesus Christ" (*Enchiridion of Indulgences*, no. 63).

Prayer of St Catherine Siena

(which may be prayed before making the Way of the Cross)

O Eternal Truth! What is Thy teaching and by what way must we follow to come to Thy Father? I know no other than that which Thou hast traced by Thy Precious Blood and which Thou hast affirmed by the admirable virtues of Thy ardent charity. It is our way today, O abyss of charity! I implore Thy mercy, give me the grace to follow Thy teaching with a simple heart; grant me a continual desire to suffer whatever pains come my way for Thy sake. Give to my eyes, O my Jesus, fountains of tears, that I may obtain Thy mercy for the whole world and above all for Thy Spouse the Church. I have sinned, O Lord, have pity on me. Amen.

First Station: Jesus is Condemned to Death

V: We adore Thee, O Christ, and we bless Thee.
R: Because by Thy Holy Cross Thou hast redeemed the world.

Purge me with hyssop and I shall be clean;
wash me and I shall be whiter than snow.
(*Ps* 51:7)

Seated on the judgement seat, Pilate, though guilty of sin as all men are, judges the only truly Innocent One to be guilty, condemning him, who is the Life and the just Judge, to death. But who can condemn another to death? No man can have such sway over another man's life, though many powers in this world will claim this divine prerogative for themselves. Yet Pilate, dressed in blood red, executes God's power of life and death over another, claiming for the state the blood of the man who is God.

Ad Te omnis caro véniet, as the opening verses of the Requiem Mass goes – to you all flesh will come with its burden of sin (see *Ps* 65:2-3). So, in his flesh and sacred humanity, Christ our God has willed to carry the burden of our sins. For, coming forth from the Father and becoming man "for us men and for our salvation", Christ's exodus has taken him to this crisis point. Now he shall return to the Father, going to him along the way of the cross, bearing the burden of our sin that weighs upon his tortured flesh.

Although his hands are bound, Christ freely chooses this way of love, thus showing us the costliness of our Christian dignity. Indeed, he has weighed the inalienable worth of every human life and judged us to be worthy of redemption. And so, with the freedom of love, Jesus chooses to suffer and shed his life-giving blood for love of us, so that with every step of the journey to which he is consigned by Pilate he, our God, can cleanse and wash us of our sin and guilt. Indeed, he alone can wash and absolve Pilate of his guilt. For though our sins are scarlet, as Pilate's robe is, we shall become white as wool (see *Is* 1:18). For the Good Shepherd has thus called us to follow him into his green pastures.

All: *Our Father... Hail Mary... Glory be to the Father...*

I love Thee Jesus, my love above all things. I repent with my whole heart for having offended Thee. Never permit me to separate myself from Thee again. Grant that I may love Thee always, and then do with me what Thou wilt.

Second Station: The Wood of the Cross is Laid Upon Jesus

V: We adore Thee, O Christ, and we bless Thee.
R: Because by Thy Holy Cross Thou hast redeemed the world.

Surely he has borne our griefs and carried our sorrows; yet we esteemed him stricken, smitten by God, and afflicted.
(*Is* 53:4)

Our griefs and our sorrows stem from sin: the sin of the world, its structures and its powerbrokers; the sins inflicted upon us; and the sins we commit, inflicting sorrow and grief upon others, and for ourselves. All these Jesus bears upon his broad shoulders which are already lacerated and bruised and bleeding. Yet love gives Jesus strength of will and body to do this, taking the rough wood of the heavy cross upon himself. With serenity, therefore, Jesus accepts the wood of the cross. As Isaiah says: "He was oppressed, and he was afflicted, yet he opened not his mouth" (*Is* 53:7).

As a shepherd carries the lost sheep upon his shoulders, so now Jesus carries the sins of the world, represented by the cross, a brutal instrument of torture. Christ does this so that humanity, lost through original sin, is now found; man's sins are forgiven through this journey of love that the Good Shepherd willingly and peacefully undertakes for us. Out of love for us, Christ also becomes the Lamb and the Sacrifice that takes away our griefs and sorrows, restoring peace between God and man. So great is the power of God's love to renew and purify all creation that the wood of the cross becomes no longer a thing of shame and humiliation, but an object of veneration: *Ecce lignum crucis*! "Behold the wood of the cross, on which hung the salvation of the world," we sing on Good Friday. The saving love of God, thus revealed, is so precious, so beautiful, so long-desired that, in the radiant light of salvation, even the sin of Adam is seen in a new perspective. *O felix culpa*, we declare in the dark night of Easter, standing in the light of the Paschal candle: "O happy fault that earned for us so great, so glorious a Redeemer!"

Jesus refers to his passion, to this way of the cross, as his "hour of glory" (see *Jn* 12:23). The word for 'glory' in Hebrew, *kavod*, also has the sense of something weighty, heavy, that is being laid upon someone. The cross, therefore, heavy and burdensome, is the *kavod*, the glory now being laid upon Jesus. Glorious indeed is the weight of the cross, for through it the sin of man that has burdened all of creation and brought mankind low is now lifted from us; glorious indeed is this wood, stained crimson with the blood that washes away our sins, on which hung the salvation of the world.

All: *Our Father… Hail Mary… Glory be to the Father…*

I love Thee Jesus, my love above all things. I repent with my whole heart for having offended Thee. Never permit me to separate myself from Thee again. Grant that I may love Thee always, and then do with me what Thou wilt.

Third Station: Jesus Falls the First Time Under the Weight of the Cross

V: We adore Thee, O Christ, and we bless Thee.
R: Because by Thy Holy Cross Thou hast redeemed the world.

But he was wounded for our transgressions,
he was bruised for our iniquities;
upon him was the chastisement that made us whole.
(*Is* 53:5)

Thrice, as the cross is revealed in the Good Friday liturgy, do we genuflect and venerate its wood. So, too, on his journey to Calvary, three times does Christ's body succumb to the weight of the cross; he is chastised to make us whole.

Jesus is depicted as though genuflecting beneath the cross, his first fall. For his three falls, these three genuflections of the Lord under the weight of our sins, we can make reparation by genuflecting before the cross, not only during the lengthy Good Friday liturgy, but also in this devotional Way of the Cross. Looking upon the image of him who humbled himself under the cross, weighed down by this instrument of humiliation and death, so we too shall humble ourselves before God, going down on one knee. For just as St Peter denied the Lord thrice and was then asked thrice if he loved Jesus, thus allowing Peter a chance to make reparation for his sin, so we too are invited by the Church's liturgy and in this devotion of the *via crucis* to show our love, our reverence, our adoration of the Lord who, for love of us, bent his knees under the weight of the cross.

Our Lord allows himself to succumb to the weight of the cross because he wants to share in our human weaknesses and redeem us from them. His three falls, perhaps, will correspond to the three powers of the human soul that can lead us astray. These three powers of the human soul are the intellect, or our thoughts and ideas; the will, or our desires and wants; and the passions, or our emotions and feelings. Through his first fall and then lovingly rising up again, Jesus saves us from sins of the intellect: intellectual pride – the tendency to think we know best, or to use our knowledge and learning to dominate others – or perhaps the not using the reasoning mind that God has given us and tending towards lazy thinking, superstition, or mindlessly following popular opinions and ideas and political trends even if they contradict the Word of God.

So, genuflecting before the Lord, we confess our sins of the intellect; we repent of them; we make reparation for them through this act of humility; and we rise again with our loving and merciful Saviour.

All: *Our Father... Hail Mary... Glory be to the Father...*

I love Thee Jesus, my love above all things. I repent with my whole heart for having offended Thee. Never permit me to separate myself from Thee again. Grant that I may love Thee always, and then do with me what Thou wilt.

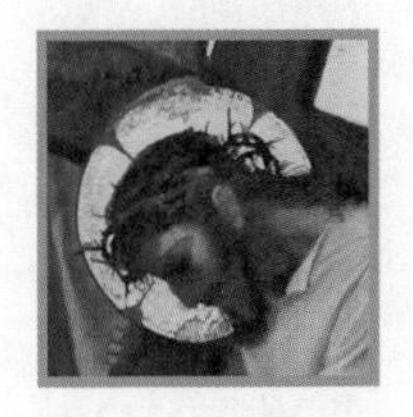

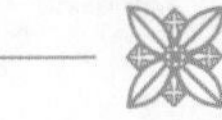

Fourth Station: Jesus Meets His Grieving Mother

V: We adore Thee, O Christ, and we bless Thee.
R: Because by Thy Holy Cross Thou hast redeemed the world.

There your mother was in travail with you,
there she who bore you was in travail.
(*Sg* 8:5)

From this point onwards, Mary accompanies her beloved son right to the very end, to the grave and even to the Resurrection, for pious traditions would hold that Mary was the first, even before St Mary Magdalene, to meet the risen Lord. Nevertheless, in these stations painted for a Marian shrine, the Mother of God is eminently present, standing by Jesus until he is placed in the garden tomb.

For according to the prophecy of Simeon, Christ "is set for the fall and rising of many in Israel, and for a sign that is spoken against (and a sword will pierce through your own soul also)" (*Lk* 2:34-35). So, Mary shall share in Jesus's rejection and suffering. In this regard, Mary is surely like every good mother. For which loving mother has not followed and vigilantly watched over her child in his or her suffering and illness: sitting by the bedside; going to the hospital at all hours; grieving, weeping and mourning with each sad diagnosis and mishap that befalls her sweet child.

Mary, in this station, represents every true mother, then, and any parent who has loved a child will know the pain that Mary endures, and she shares in theirs. "Grief is the price we pay for love," the late Queen Elizabeth II, a mother of four, had rightly said. For only a heart that loves will feel so keenly the sufferings of the beloved – it is like a sword that pierces the soul – and the immaculate heart of Mary who loves so purely will also feel more intensely than we can the purest agony of grief as she meets her sinless son bent over by the heavy cross of our iniquities.

But he looks up and sees Mary; his eyes of mercy meets hers, and the son says to the mother, the Virgin Bride: "Behold, I make all things new" (see *Rv* 21:5). Mary is the image of the Church, the mother of all Christians, and so with these words God addresses you and me too. God is making all things new through his love, which is stronger than death, which no floods of destruction can drown nor extinguish (see *Sg* 8:6, 7). Christ's gaze of love, therefore, gives Mary a glimpse of the Resurrection, and so he comforts her in her grief and encourages her to walk this way of love with him. So, too, for us.

Christ meets us on the way of the cross in our lives, and he looks upon us with love, encouraging us to daily take up our cross and follow him (see *Mt* 16:24). With Mary our Mother, we follow him, knowing that Christ is ever present with us bearing the cross with us. For as St Paul says: "Love bears all things, believes all things, hopes all things, endures all things" (*1 Co* 13:7).

All: *Our Father… Hail Mary… Glory be to the Father…*

I love Thee Jesus, my love above all things. I repent with my whole heart for having offended Thee. Never permit me to separate myself from Thee again. Grant that I may love Thee always, and then do with me what Thou wilt.

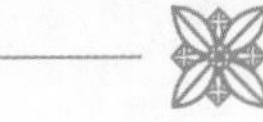

Fifth Station:
Jesus is Helped by Simon of Cyrene in the Carrying of the Cross

V: We adore Thee, O Christ, and we bless Thee.
R: Because by Thy Holy Cross Thou hast redeemed the world.

As they went out, they came upon a man of Cyrene,
Simon by name; this man they compelled to carry his cross.
(*Mt* 27:32)

Jesus has said that anyone who wants to be a disciple of his must daily pick up his cross and follow him. But often we might feel compelled to carry the cross: in an instant, unexpected illness and tragedy can strike us, and personal disasters and social calamities in which we can be caught up can shatter all our plans and disrupt our lives. We might resign ourselves to our new realities, and we can take up the cross laid upon us, but more often than not, we feel that this is a cross we have been forced to endure – perhaps with humiliation, resentment or anger such as might have been felt by Simon of Cyrene.

Although Simon is said to be helping Jesus, in fact Jesus can help us to carry our crosses if, in faith, we consider this: God is with us. Seldom, then, is Simon shown leading the way, but rather Christ still leads us down the way of the cross, carrying the heavier front of the cross, and leading us on the way of his saving love.

A wise and holy priest who mentored me when I was a seminarian was diagnosed with motor neurone disease: an active and energetic man cut down in his prime. In one of my last telephone conversations with him he told me: "I just ask the Lord to show me how I am to be faithful to the vocation he's given me in these new circumstances."

So, like Simon, we can be going our way on a particular journey, then suddenly diverted and made to carry a cross which seems not to be ours. However, in our new circumstances, with unfamiliar crosses, we can pray to the Lord to show us how we can be faithful to our fundamental vocation of love; we can be shown his way of sacrificial love; and we can follow him still. Christ's wordless invitation – and it is his silence that can be most hard to bear – is just to step into his footprints and follow him who has gone before us even into the grave and beyond. And love is stronger than death. Hence, Moses told Joshua as he went into the Promised Land: "It is the Lord who goes before you; he will be with you, he will not fail you or forsake you; do not fear or be dismayed" (*Dt* 31:8).

The strong love of Christ helps and transforms Simon so that his resentment turns into acceptance and into a true sharing in the redeeming work of Christ. Thus, Simon's own sons Alexander and Rufus, who are onlookers, are said to have become missionaries and leaders among the early Christians.

All: *Our Father… Hail Mary… Glory be to the Father…*

I love Thee Jesus, my love above all things. I repent with my whole heart for having offended Thee. Never permit me to separate myself from Thee again. Grant that I may love Thee always, and then do with me what Thou wilt.

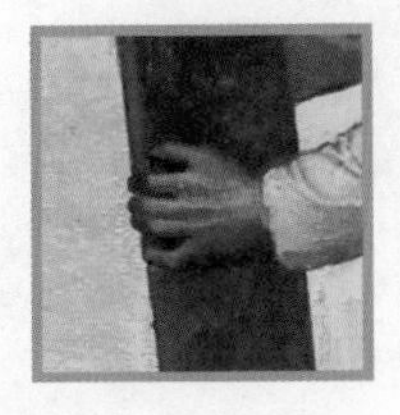

Sixth Station: Jesus is Cleaned with the Face Cloth of Veronica

V: We adore Thee, O Christ, and we bless Thee.
R: Because by Thy Holy Cross Thou hast redeemed the world.

He had no form or comeliness that we should look at him,
and no beauty that we should desire him…
and as one from whom men hide their faces
he was despised, and we esteemed him not.
(*Is* 53:2b, 3b)

Veronica's name means 'true icon', because, as we see, she carries a perfect image of Christ's holy face imprinted on her handkerchief or face cloth. However, this holy woman is rightly called the *vera ikon*, because, by her compassion and her courageous act of love and mercy shown to the suffering Jesus, she is a true image of Christ our God who has bent down in compassion through the Incarnation to wash our faces clean of sin by the shedding of his blood.

Indeed, humanity has been disfigured by sin such that the beauty of God in whose image man has been made is obscured and marred. It is man, fallen into sin, who has lost the grace that was given to our first parents. And so, it is sinful humanity who "had no beauty that we should desire him". Sin also sadly blinds us, so that we do not see the humanity of the other person, the sanctity of every human life, and the dignity of man that comes from God our Father and Creator.

So, Christ comes to show us that despite our disfigurement by sin, God still desires us. God desires friendship with us even when we have turned away from him; when the Devil, that unholy brigand, has stripped us of grace and robbed us of our human dignity, leaving us half dead by the wayside (see *Lk* 10:30b), our God comes to us in great compassion and lifts us up and places us within his holy inn, the Church, so that by the grace of the sacraments we can be healed and re-fashioned in the image and likeness of Christ the Son. God desires that our faces and our lives should be so transformed by his grace that we shall have the beauty of Christ and become true icons of him, with faces that shine with compassion in a world that is lonely and dark.

Hence, Jesus walks this way of love, going down the road out of Jerusalem, and those who are on the wayside and who will look at his holy face will be transformed and saved. Many, who despise him, hide their faces from him, just as many now will not look on the face of the beggar, the stranger, the drug-addict, the prisoner, the most vulnerable and in need on our streets. But for those who do look and see – and who will esteem the other as a fellow man and so bridge the divide of inhumanity by reaching out in love and compassion – these, like St Veronica, are true icons of Jesus Christ. And this, of course, is our baptismal vocation, as we carry the holy face imprinted not on cloth but on our hearts and minds.

All: *Our Father… Hail Mary… Glory be to the Father…*

I love Thee Jesus, my love above all things. I repent with my whole heart for having offended Thee. Never permit me to separate myself from Thee again. Grant that I may love Thee always, and then do with me what Thou wilt.

Seventh Station: Jesus Falls Again Under the Weight of the Cross

V: We adore Thee, O Christ, and we bless Thee.
R: Because by Thy Holy Cross Thou hast redeemed the world.

My strength is dried up like a potsherd,
and my tongue cleaves to my jaws;
thou dost lay me in the dust of death.
(*Ps* 22:15)

Christ falls to his knees again, and this time both his knees will strike the rocky ground, as clouds of dust send specks into his eyes and cake his raw wounds with dirt. Adam, the first man, whose name means 'earth' or 'ground', had been formed from the clay of the earth, and God had breathed life into him. Now Christ is covered with dirt and dust that mixes with his lacerated flesh so that he looks like a new man of the clay, the second Adam. He breathes heavily under the weight of the cross, breathing new life into the old creation with every momentous step of this way of the cross, this way of revivifying love.

Through this second fall, Christ redeems us from the sins of our weak human wills into which we fall repeatedly, often against our better judgement. For an effect of original sin is the disharmony between our reason and our wills. As St Paul put it so strikingly: "I can will what is right, but I cannot do it. For I do not do the good I want, but the evil I do not want is what I do" (*Rm* 7:18b-19). Often our resolutions for the good crumble as our wills veer towards familiar sins and temptations; often we choose poorly and we cannot find the strength of will to stand up for the good, for the faith, for justice, and to do what we know to be right. St Paul thus exclaims: "Wretched man that I am! Who will deliver me from this body of death?" (*Rm* 7:24)

Christ delivers us by his passion and cross. Christ, who has been tempted like us in all things but did not sin, empathises and is our example of fortitude and our source of strength and grace. By his second fall, Christ kneels beside us when we have fallen into sin once again, into habitual sins, and urges us not to despair but rather to look at him and hope in the power of grace and in the power of his love to heal and save us.

Christ therefore clings resolutely to the cross, his will and his purpose unbent even as his body is bent over under the weight of those blessed beams. We too, fixing our eyes on Jesus, can rise with him, and continue to walk to Calvary, clinging to our cross which Christ bears with us, and following him to the end. As St Paul says: "There is therefore now no condemnation for those who are in Christ Jesus" (*Rm* 8:1).

All: *Our Father… Hail Mary… Glory be to the Father…*

I love Thee Jesus, my love above all things. I repent with my whole heart for having offended Thee. Never permit me to separate myself from Thee again. Grant that I may love Thee always, and then do with me what Thou wilt.

Eighth Station:
Jesus Speaks to the Weeping Women

V: We adore Thee, O Christ, and we bless Thee.
R: Because by Thy Holy Cross Thou hast redeemed the world.

And there followed him a great multitude of the people,
and of women who bewailed and lamented him.
But Jesus turning to them said,
"Daughters of Jerusalem, do not weep for me,
but weep for yourselves and for your children".
(*Lk* 23:27-28)

The women weep for Jesus; they lament his unjust condemnation, his truly innocent death. Perhaps they were among the crowds who heard him preaching and teaching, and they had hung upon his words because he taught them with authority (see *Mt* 7:29). So now, Jesus teaches them once more.

The look on Christ's face is one of sorrow, a haunted expression as he foresees the destruction that will befall Jerusalem just over a generation later. The women now approaching him will be old, but their children and their children's children will live to see the siege and conquest of Jerusalem by Roman forces. Christ is not impassive in the face of the tragedy that befalls mankind, over and over again because of the violence, cruelty and inhumanity that we mete out to one another. Such is the lot of the old Jerusalem, the way of widespread suffering and warring princes, which the Lord shares as he journeys to his barbaric execution. Therefore, God is with us in all the conflicts and terrors and brutalities that have befallen men and women down through the generations to our day, and Jesus weeps for us.

What, then, does Jesus teach the weeping women? What word has he for us now? "Weep for yourselves and for your children." Jesus is thus calling us to contrition: to be sorrowful for our sins; to have sorrow and compunction for the sins of the world; and to weep for the conversion of sinners. Thus St Dominic, our holy founder, would every night do penance for sins, crying out to the Lord: "My God, my mercy, what will become of sinners?"

Earlier in St Luke's Gospel, Jesus is confronted with another tragedy – the collapse of the tower of Siloam in Jerusalem – and he at once calls the people to repentance: "Unless you repent you will all likewise perish" (*Lk* 13:5). But this is the Saviour's desire: by believing in him, we "should not perish but have eternal life" (see *Jn* 3:16).

Standing and facing the weeping multitudes – and therefore facing us, Jesus invites us to believe in him, and to follow him up to the new Jerusalem, the new heavens and the new earth where he shall "wipe away every tear from their eyes" (*Rv* 21:4).

All: *Our Father... Hail Mary... Glory be to the Father...*

I love Thee Jesus, my love above all things. I repent with my whole heart for having offended Thee. Never permit me to separate myself from Thee again. Grant that I may love Thee always, and then do with me what Thou wilt.

Ninth Station: Jesus Falls the Third Time Under the Weight of the Cross

V: We adore Thee, O Christ, and we bless Thee.
R: Because by Thy Holy Cross Thou hast redeemed the world.

I have sewed sackcloth upon my skin,
and have laid my strength in the dust.
My face is red with weeping,
and on my eyelids is deep darkness.
(*Jb* 16:15-16)

How often have we fallen into the same sins repeatedly? Overcome by our emotions, by our passions and bad habits, by our cravings and aversions, we fall into sinful patterns of behaviour, addicted to the very acts and the kinds of things that we know will not help us in the long run, but which we feel we need in that moment of weakness. The Lord knows how deflated and defeated we can feel when habitual sin keeps pulling us down.

Crushed by the weight of the cross, Christ falls a third time, exhausted by the burden of our sins; prone on the hard earth, he joins us in our place of dejection and disappointment where we have struggled against sin but seem to fall repeatedly into a hard and lonely place.

St Paul, however, says that "for our sake God made him [Jesus] to be sin who knew no sin" (*2 Co* 5:21), so although he was without sin, Jesus knows our fallen human condition, he knows intimately our struggles, our temptations and our weaknesses. He knows, too, the oppressive power of sin and its attraction, like the wood of the cross pressing down on his aching body.

We might feel exhausted by the struggle against sin, especially after decades of trying to be rid of it. Perhaps we are tired by the repeated cycle of confession and relapse. Perhaps we feel despair and cannot find the strength to carry on.

But we are not alone in this dark place. Flat on the unforgiving ground, tried and found wanting, we need only open our eyes and see that our merciful Saviour is right there with us. He wants to raise us up and redeem us from our feelings, which are often transient, and which, by their vehemence, can lead us astray. By his third fall, therefore, Christ saves us from the sins of our passions; he saves us with the truth of who God is: God is love, and his mercy is without end. Hence Pope Francis says: "Never forget this: the Lord never gets tired of forgiving us. It is we who get tired of asking for forgiveness."

The Lord's body is now exhausted by the journey he has taken from the Praetorium. But his spirit is undaunted, because his love and mercy for sinners never tires nor relents. Indeed, as St Paul says, Christ has become sin for us, suffered for us and with us, "so that in him we might become the righteousness of God" (*2 Co* 5:21). This motive gives Jesus strength to stay on this way of love.

All: *Our Father... Hail Mary... Glory be to the Father...*

I love Thee Jesus, my love above all things. I repent with my whole heart for having offended Thee. Never permit me to separate myself from Thee again. Grant that I may love Thee always, and then do with me what Thou wilt.

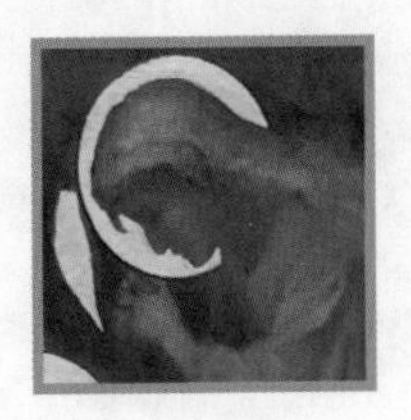

Tenth Station: Jesus is Stripped of His Clothing

V: We adore Thee, O Christ, and we bless Thee.
R: Because by Thy Holy Cross Thou hast redeemed the world.

I can count all my bones – they stare and gloat over me;
they divide my garments among them,
and for my raiment they cast lots.
(*Ps* 22:17-18)

Christ the second Adam stands naked as the first Adam had been at the time of his creation; thus divested, Christ will inaugurate the new creation. There is for Christ, the Innocent One, no shame in this, just as our first parents before their fall into sin did not notice nor feel ashamed by their own nakedness. However, the soldiers who strip Jesus clearly do this to humiliate him, to gloat at him, and to invite the jeers of passers-by.

If one visits the former Nazi extermination camp at Auschwitz, one sees in the museum piles and piles of clothing – leather shoes, spectacles, coats, jackets, shirts – and also sacks full of human hair. For clothing typically dignifies the human being, just as hair is an adornment. Clothes are sometimes used to indicate our identity and role in life, and mark special occasions and functions; as such they are deeply humanising artefacts. The Nazis, therefore, stripped their victims of their clothing to deepen their shame and to rob them of their identity and their jobs – even their humanity, as they were then mass exterminated in a callous manner that was not even befitting of beasts.

It is a chilling and haunting experience to wander through the rooms in Auschwitz and see the piles of clothing and ponder the lives wrenched from these poor people and left behind in this way, behind glass cases in a museum where once they had wandered the corridors or been incarcerated.

As Jesus is stripped of his garments, so he stands alongside the many people of every generation who have been stripped of their human dignity and deprived of their inherent worth, people who have been abused and tortured and shamed, people who have been degraded and mocked by other human beings. Christ knows their humiliation and pain, and through his way of the cross, Christ restores to us our human dignity. For to every man, Christ our God says, "You are my beloved Son, my beloved Daughter, and you are worth dying for. For you and for your salvation, I became man and took on the condition of a slave, even accepting death on the Cross. Naked I came from my mother's womb, and naked shall I return; blessed be the name of the Lord!" (see *Jb* 1:21).

All: *Our Father... Hail Mary... Glory be to the Father...*

I love Thee Jesus, my love above all things. I repent with my whole heart for having offended Thee. Never permit me to separate myself from Thee again. Grant that I may love Thee always, and then do with me what Thou wilt.

Eleventh Station:
Jesus is Affixed with Nails to the Cross

V: We adore Thee, O Christ, and we bless Thee.
R: Because by Thy Holy Cross Thou hast redeemed the world.

A company of evildoers encircle me;
they have pierced my hands and feet (*Ps* 22:16).

Sinful man is accustomed to doing things by violence and force, acting against the will of another. God however, having endowed us with the divine gift of freedom and a will to choose and love, never forces us and does not condone violence in the things of religion. He wills that we should freely love him, and, freely choosing the good, should act accordingly, with sacrificial love.

When the soldiers came to arrest Jesus in the garden of Gethsemane, they came with ropes and weapons, threatening Jesus and his apostles and binding him up with rope to take him to Caiaphas. Wondering at their violence, the Lord said to them: "Have you come out as against a robber, with swords and clubs? When I was with you day after day in the temple, you did not lay hands on me. But this is your hour, and the power of darkness" (*Lk* 22:52b-53). For the Son of God became man and freely shared our human nature out of love, obedient to the Father's will which is, likewise, the same loving will to save humanity from the powers of darkness. For this work, Christ needed no ropes nor weapons nor compulsion. Rather, he had in love given his all to the Father's plan for our salvation: "Not my will, but thine, be done" (*Lk* 22:42).

Therefore, when the time came for Christ to be crucified, the nails were not necessary to fix him to the cross. But in order that the prophecies might be fulfilled, the Son of God is pierced with nails. In order to satisfy the cruelty of his executioners, the bloodlust of man through the ages, the Son of Man has nails driven through his hands and feet. And in order to share in the excruciating pain that we human beings sometimes have to undergo, Jesus Christ also wills to be crucified. Hence St Paul said: "Christ redeemed us from the curse of the law, having become a curse for us – for it is written, 'Cursed be every one who hangs on a tree'" (*Ga* 3:13).

Jesus, therefore, although he is pierced with nails, is transfixed to the cross not by these harsh shards of cold iron, but rather he is held to the cross and remains on the cross, that instrument of our salvation, through the ardour of his love. As St Catherine of Siena said: "Nails would not be enough to hold God-and-Man nailed and fastened on the cross had Love not held him there."

All: *Our Father… Hail Mary… Glory be to the Father…*

I love Thee Jesus, my love above all things. I repent with my whole heart for having offended Thee. Never permit me to separate myself from Thee again. Grant that I may love Thee always, and then do with me what Thou wilt.

INRI

Twelfth Station: Jesus Dies on the Cross

V: We adore Thee, O Christ, and we bless Thee.
R: Because by Thy Holy Cross Thou hast redeemed the world.

After this Jesus, knowing that all was now finished,
said (to fulfil the scripture), "I thirst." ...
When Jesus had received the vinegar, he said,
"It is finished"; and he bowed his head and gave up his spirit.
(*Jn* 19:28, 30)

Every chapel of the Missionaries of Charity, that admirable religious congregation founded by St Teresa of Kolkata, has these words of Jesus, "I thirst", inscribed next to the large crucifix that hangs behind the altar. In 1946 St Teresa clearly heard Jesus telling her: "I thirst for you, for your love"; she understood that she and all those who would join her congregation were called to satisfy as much as they could the thirst of Jesus for their love. By walking this way of the cross today, by our prayers and tears as we follow the Lord in his passion, we can give to Jesus our love, and so become in that way little missionaries of charity, sent out in love to bring love to Christ. And we might remember that Christ, the suffering Christ, is found in the least, in the most vulnerable and needy, in the poorest of the poor all around us. Every day, and not only in Lent, we are sent out as missionaries of charity to satisfy their thirst, to give them the love we have received from God.

If we become missionaries of charity in this way, and we learn to pour out our lives in service of the poor, in care and love for those in need; if we seek Christ in those around us, then we can truly say with the Lord that "it is finished". This is to say that Christ's redeeming work has been accomplished.

For Christ has died in order that man might live, in order to give us a share in his divine life, and God is love. When we have been raised up from the deadliness of our sins, and revived by the power of Christ's cross, then we shall love as Christ loves, alive in his Holy Spirit. Then we shall know that God's saving work is being carried out in us; then the saving work he finished on the cross is having its desired effect in this world, for he is renewing his creation through divine love.

As we gaze upon the Crucified One now, let us kneel and pray that we will have the strength and courage and wisdom to satisfy his thirst today; let us pray that the Spirit whom Christ has poured forth from the cross will make us receive new life, and become on fire with his love.

St John says: "By this we know love, that he laid down his life for us; and we ought to lay down our lives for the brethren. But if any one has the world's goods and sees his brother in need, yet closes his heart against him, how does God's love abide in him? Little children, let us not love in word or speech but in deed and in truth" (*1 Jn* 3:16-18).

All: *Our Father… Hail Mary… Glory be to the Father…*

I love Thee Jesus, my love above all things. I repent with my whole heart for having offended Thee. Never permit me to separate myself from Thee again. Grant that I may love Thee always, and then do with me what Thou wilt.

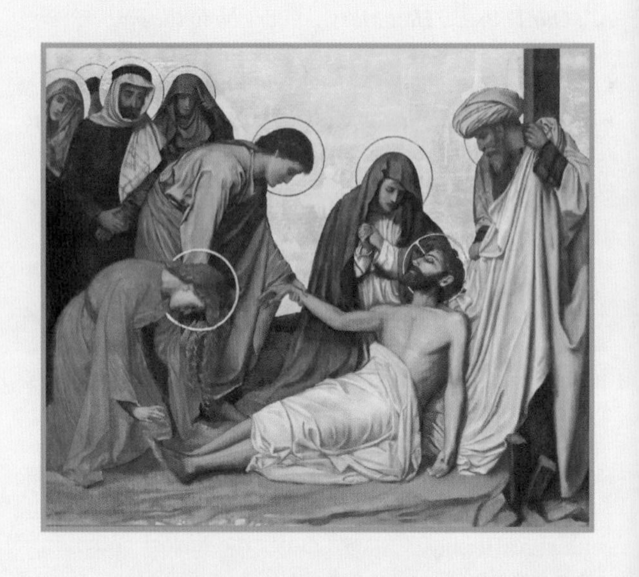

Thirteenth Station: Jesus is Taken Down from the Cross

V: We adore Thee, O Christ, and we bless Thee.
R: Because by Thy Holy Cross Thou hast redeemed the world.

And when [Pilate] learned from the centurion that he was dead, he granted the body to Joseph [of Arimathea]. And he bought a linen shroud, and taking him down, wrapped him in the linen shroud.
(*Mk* 15:45-46)

Just over three decades earlier, Mary had borne God in her womb, given birth to the Lord of Life himself, wrapped him in linen swaddling bands, and cradled him against her body, holding the baby Jesus close in the intimate darkness of a shelter hewn from living rock, a cave in Bethlehem. Now, in the darkness of the strange eclipse that has come over the land, as the rock itself has come alive with a sudden earthquake, Mary cradles the lifeless body of the adult Jesus, who is wrapped again in linen cloths.

How the Virgin's Immaculate Heart must have broken at this point, and yet Mary united her sorrows and sufferings with those of Christ Crucified because she knew that her son had to be "about his Father's business" (*Lk* 2:49), doing the Father's work of redemption. For the way of love had led Jesus, begotten from before all ages of the Father's heart, to this point, and Mary had walked with him every step of the way. And now she lies there on the ground, in the shadow of the cross, cradling her son. Her heart, which had beaten in tandem with Jesus's, now beats alone; Christ's Sacred Heart has been stopped.

For the immaculate Virgin, this must have been a moment of great isolation: her most chaste spouse had died some years before, and now her sinless son has gone too, leaving her in a darkened world as the light of life is snuffed out, and the power of darkness seems triumphant. For those who are striving for virtue, who are trying to live the Christian life in this world, sometimes we too can feel quite alone and isolated and surrounded by opposition.

However, as St John wrote: "the light shines in the darkness, and the darkness has not overcome it" (*Jn* 1:5). The kindness of a stranger, a secret follower of Jesus like Joseph of Arimathea who made all the practical arrangements to have Jesus's body recovered and buried, is such a light in the darkness. So too is the presence of St John and St Mary Magdalene, faithful followers and friends of Jesus who would now care for Mary. In our world, kindness, friendship and love are signs, coming from the disciples of Christ in our time, that the light of God's grace, his love, still shines in the darkness. And the darkness shall not overcome it.

With Mary, therefore, we are called to keep faith, to endure the darkness and the loneliness temporarily, just for part of this brief lifetime. For Mary's faith in the promises of God and in the words of her son would lead her to know that death is not the end. Through her prayers, may we too have the light of such faith in dark and desolate times.

All: *Our Father... Hail Mary... Glory be to the Father...*

I love Thee Jesus, my love above all things. I repent with my whole heart for having offended Thee. Never permit me to separate myself from Thee again. Grant that I may love Thee always, and then do with me what Thou wilt.

Fourteenth Station: Jesus is Buried in the Sepulchre

V: We adore Thee, O Christ, and we bless Thee.
R: Because by Thy Holy Cross Thou hast redeemed the world.

And they made his grave with the wicked
and with a rich man in his death,
although he had done no violence,
and there was no deceit in his mouth.
(*Is* 53:9)

The psalmist says: "Where shall I go from thy Spirit? Or where shall I flee from thy presence? If I ascend to heaven, thou art there! If I make my bed in Sheol, thou art there! … If I say, 'Let only darkness cover me, and the light about me be night', even the darkness is not dark to thee, the night is bright as the day; for darkness is as light with thee" (*Ps* 139:7-8, 11-12). So the Lord of Life, out of his great love for us, wills even to descend into the grave, into Sheol, into the shadowy realms of the dead, fulfilling the Scripture. Even in the grave, God is present; even in death God is with us!

Christ is buried in the sepulchre, a new rock-hewn tomb, lent by a rich man, in a garden just metres from Calvary, so close that it is within sight of the place of the crucifixion.

A great stone is rolled over the mouth of the tomb, and then, within, all is silent and still.

Total silence and stillness are something foreign to many of us in our time. Yet Christ often sought God in silence, in deserted places. And the prophet Elijah encountered God not, as he expected, in earthquake, wind and fire, but in stillness and, as the Hebrew text puts it, "in the sound of a soft silence" (see *1 K* 19:12). But all too often, when we pray, or when we cry out to God in our need, it seems as if we are met only with silence, with the non-response of the *Deus absconditus*, the hidden and inscrutable God (see *Is* 45:15); we are met, it seems, with the silence of a cold and frightening tomb.

"Where is God?" people wonder. However, in this station we contemplate Christ placed into the grave. Entering the silence of the stone-cold tomb, therefore, God is present to meet us in the silences that we have to endure. Even in the grave, even in the silence, even in death, God is there.

And the response of the psalmist to this revelation is that where God is, then even "the darkness is as light". For, in faith, we know that the sepulchre, ultimately, is silent – not because it is all death and devoid of life, but because it is empty; it could not contain Love himself. Yes, the silence of the empty tomb will eventually prove that love is stronger than death (see *Sg* 8:6). Having followed Christ on this way of love, may we be led all the way to share with him in life unending. Amen.

All: *Our Father… Hail Mary… Glory be to the Father…*

I love Thee Jesus, my love above all things. I repent with my whole heart for having offended Thee. Never permit me to separate myself from Thee again. Grant that I may love Thee always, and then do with me what Thou wilt.

Concluding prayer

(said before a crucifix)

Look down upon me, good and gentle Jesus, while before Thy face I humbly kneel, and with burning soul I pray and beseech Thee to fix deep in my heart lively sentiments of faith, hope and charity, true contrition for my sins, and a firm purpose of amendment; while I contemplate with great love and tender pity Thy five wounds, pondering over them within me, having in mind the words which David Thy prophet said of Thee, my Jesus: "They have pierced my hands and my feet; they have numbered all my bones." Amen.

Note: "A plenary indulgence is granted on each Friday of Lent and Passiontide to the faithful who, after Communion, piously recite the above prayer before an image of Christ Crucified; on other days of the year the indulgence is partial" (*Enchiridion of Indulgences*, no. 22).

INRI

CANTICLE
of the
PASSION

S: CATH: RICC:

The Origin of the Canticle

The verses on the following pages, compiled from scripture, were given to St Catherine de Ricci, a cloistered Dominican tertiary – our modern-day equivalent of apostolic Sisters – who lived in a convent in Florence in the sixteenth century. For a period of twelve years, St Catherine de Ricci experienced all the pains of Christ's passion, suffering with him every week, from noon on Thursday until late afternoon on Friday. After the first of these mystical experiences, when she had received the sacred stigmata, Our Lady appeared to St Catherine and told her that she now understood and shared in Mary's own sufferings as she stood by the cross of her son. Hence, she gave this compilation, called the 'Canticle of the Passion', to St Catherine and asked her to meditate on it, and so continue to grow in love for the crucified Lord Jesus. It became a tradition in the Dominican Order, and especially in the convents of enclosed Dominican nuns, to pray these verses every Friday in Lent.

My friends and my kinsmen
have approached and stood against me.
I was betrayed and I went not out.
My eyes have languished for weariness.
And my sweat has become
like drops of blood trickling down upon the earth.
Many dogs have surrounded me.
The council of the wicked has besieged me.
I gave my body to the scourgers
and my cheeks to be smitten.
I turned not away my face from those who
upbraided me
and spat upon me –
because I am prepared for scourging
and my sorrow is ever before me.
The soldiers plaiting a crown of thorns
have placed it upon my head.
They have pierced my hands and my feet;
they have numbered all my bones.
And they gave me gall for food,
and in my thirst they gave me vinegar to drink.
All who saw me derided me;
they spoke with their lips, and wagged the head.
They have looked upon me and watched me;
they divided my vestments among them
and upon my vesture they cast lots.
Into thy hands I commend my spirit.

Thou hast redeemed me, O Lord, God of truth.
Remember thy servants, O Lord,
when thou comest into thy kingdom.

But Jesus, crying with a loud voice,
gave up his spirit.

The mercies of the Lord
I will sing forever.
Surely he hath borne our infirmities
and carried our sorrows.
He was wounded for our iniquities;
he was bruised for our sins.
All we like sheep have gone astray;
every one hath turned aside, into his own way.
The Lord hath laid on him
the iniquities of us all.
Arise, why sleepest thou, O Lord?
Arise and cast us not off to the end.
Behold, God is my Saviour;
I will deal confidently and will not fear.

We therefore beseech thee, O Lord, help thy servants
whom thou hast redeemed by thy precious blood.

V: Have mercy on us, O benign Jesus
R: Who hast lovingly suffered for us.

Look down, we beseech thee, O Lord, upon this thy family, for which our Lord Jesus Christ did not refuse to be delivered into the hands of the wicked and to endure the torment of the cross. We ask this through Christ our Lord, who lives and reigns with you in the unity of the Holy Spirit, God, forever and ever. Amen.

THE SEVEN LAST WORDS of OUR LORD

Holy Monday

The first word (see *Lk* 23:34):

To God, his Father:
Father, forgive them, for they know not what they do.

"Only God could love us human beings, because I certainly find it difficult!" It is so easy to think this! Look at the kinds of terrible things we are capable of. We see it every day in the news, on the streets, and in countless other atrocities taking place across the world, unseen, untold, unheard. Then there are also the sins, the hypocrisies, the injustices of which we ourselves are capable. Each of us can look within and marvel, saying "Only God could love me."

And he does. The astounding truth about God is that he loves us. He loves you. He loves those who are killed although innocent – insofar as any human being can be called innocent – in diverse places around the world. But then, he *also* loves those who do the killing, who order unspeakable atrocities, who mastermind war and who perpetrate all the other ongoing evils around the world. Yes, only God could love us human beings, even the horrible ones we would happily do without. But, thankfully, God does not think or act like us. As C.S. Lewis observes: God does not love us because we are lovable. God loves us because he *is* love.

During the fifth week of Lent, at Mass we pray the Preface of the Passion of the Lord. We hear each day:

> *[B]y the wondrous power of the cross your judgement on the world is now revealed and the authority of Christ Crucified.*

Our human sins, our violence and hatred, our killing of the innocent and our abuse of the powerless is what takes Christ to the cross. On the cross, Christ shows forth God's judgement of the world's sins, for it is our sins that have nailed him there. But it is the love of Christ for wounded sinful humanity that keeps him there. And so, when Christ judges us from the cross, his judgement and the sentence he passes upon us reveal the unfathomable love of God for human beings – and only God can love us like this.

Christ says: "Father, forgive them, for they know not what they do." Hanging on the cross, Christ is the victim of the injustice of his own people, the Jewish authorities, of the fickle bloodlust of the crowds, of the cowardice of Pilate; and he has been expertly executed, nailed to the wood of the cross, by the Roman soldiers. Almost all these people, arguably, knew what they were doing, and still did it anyhow.

And yet, what is the judgement of Christ? How does the One who is Love Incarnate speak? He says: "Father, forgive them." And then, going beyond this, he makes excuses for us: "They know not what they do." This reminds me of how a parent would speak of her young child: "Please don't mind her, she didn't know what she was doing." We often make excuses for the ones we love, usually those who are still young, immature, inexperienced, unwise – those who do not know better because of their youth or a state of mind. Christ does the same for us.

Therefore Christ, whom St John calls our 'advocate', is not only our judge but he is also our defence lawyer, pleading our case for us. The Beloved Disciple wrote: "If any one does sin, we have an advocate with the Father, Jesus Christ the righteous" (*1 Jn* 2:1). Moreover, Christ promises us that we have "another Advocate" besides him to also intercede and defend our cause, who is the Holy Spirit (*Jn* 14:16). But here on the cross we see Christ as our advocate, interceding for us, pleading our case, putting forward the mitigating circumstances for our actions: "They know not what they do."

In a fundamental, metaphysical way, this is true. On account of original sin, man is now born in what St Thomas Aquinas calls a "double darkness" of ignorance and sin – we know not what we ought to do, and even when we do know, our wills do not follow on from our reason. Many of us are familiar with this struggle, particularly during Lent, and many might even have despaired. How often do people claim that they are too far gone to come back to church or to confession? But that, of course, is what the Enemy – the Devil, who is called 'the Accuser' in the Bible – wants us to think. But what does the Lord God actually say? "Father, forgive them, for they know not what they do."

St Paul vividly describes the universal struggle with sin. He said in his letter to the Romans: "I do not understand my own actions. For I do not do what I want, but I do the very thing I hate" (*Rm* 7:15). Thus captivated by sin, St Paul then exclaims: "Wretched man that I am! Who will deliver me from this body of death?" Who, indeed, shall deliver us and set us free? The one who has the power to judge and who also is our advocate; the one who says today: "Forgive them, for they know not what they do." St Paul says, "Thanks be to God through Jesus Christ our Lord!", for St Paul knows that the struggle against sin should not end in either despair or acquiescence. Rather, unlovable though our sins make us, we must also know that God is love, and therefore loves us regardless, forgiving us even before we ask him, and longing for us to turn to him and receive his mercy, his love, and his comforting words: "They know not what they do."

I recall as a novice reading and re-reading a tantalising reflection by Fr Simon Tugwell, O.P., in which he suggests that Adam and Eve had sinned 'innocently', by which he means that they were too young, too immature, to really withstand the Enemy's temptations. J.R.R. Tolkien also refers to the race of Men as the "younger children" of the Creator of his Middle Earth. And so, in this reading of the Fall, Adam and Eve might be said to "know not what they were doing" when, doubting the wisdom and goodness of God, and swayed by the Devil's enticement of divinity, they rebelled against the One who alone can grant us a share in his divinity, and who indeed desires to do this in the fullness of time through Christ's Incarnation. Our first parents, then, imprudent in their youthfulness, fell into sin and disobedience. Perhaps our Lord hints at this mystery of original sin with these words on the cross.

But why did God permit this, then, and what about all the pain and anguish that sin brings? St Irenaeus thinks that sin is permitted so that Adam might realise as a creature that he depends on God for his all. Is this not what we are reminded of on Ash Wednesday as those ashes are sprinkled on us, a symbol of the dust from which we were made and to which we shall return? If during this Lent we have fallen and failed and fumbled and discovered how flawed we are, then perhaps this is the point: like Adam, we can realise our absolute dependence on God, our need to turn to him daily and constantly seek his mercy and grace. On a global scale, in a world that has proclaimed God to be dead, or that has declared its independence from God, perhaps the tragedies that surround us point out that we do, after all, need God.

To summarise all of this we can look to the English mystic Julian of Norwich, who, in her beautiful *Showings of Divine Love*, writes:

> [Sin] cannot be known except by the pain that is caused thereby. This pain is some thing, if I see it aright, existing for a time. For it purges us and makes us to know ourselves and to ask mercy; for the passion of our Lord is our comfort in all this – and such is his blessed will. And for the tender love that our good Lord has to all that shall be saved, he comforts them swiftly and sweetly, saying: "It is true that sin is the cause of all this pain. But all shall be well and all shall be well, and all manner of thing shall be well."

Amen!

Let us end this first meditation on the last words of Christ with the prayer that the Angel of Peace taught to the holy children of Fatima:

> *"My God, I believe, I adore, I hope and I love Thee! I ask pardon for those who do not believe, do not adore, do not hope and do not love Thee."*

Holy Tuesday

The second word (see *Lk* 23:43):

To the "good thief":
Truly, I say to you, today you will be with me in Paradise.

As Christ's first word, his first testament on the cross, is to the forgiveness that God offers to all of sinful humanity, so his second word and testimony on the cross is to particularise that forgiveness and to reveal the effect of personal repentance: it opens wide the doors of paradise. As such, Christ's words to the good thief – Saint Dismas as he is traditionally called – show us how our lives can be changed and transformed in an instant, for the spiritual action of grace takes no time at all, if we open wide our hearts to God's grace and mercy.

On most Sundays at Matins the Church prays a fourth-century hymn of thanksgiving, traditionally attributed to St Ambrose of Milan. In the central section of the hymn, we sing:

When you [Christ] became Man to set us free
you did not shun the Virgin's womb.
You overcame the sting of death
and opened the kingdom of heaven to all believers.

I.N.R.I
HODIE MECV

The first believer to whom Christ opens the kingdom of heaven is the one who says to him: "Jesus, remember me when you come into your kingdom." With these words, Dismas shows himself to be a believer: he believes that Jesus is king; that he will reign forever in a kingdom that is not of this world. Above all, he believes that Jesus will be true to his name and save him. The holy name Jesus, which the good thief calls out in prayer, means "God is my salvation". To call on the name of Jesus, therefore, is to believe in the power of God to save us through him; it is to believe in the power of Christ's advocacy. Hence the Lord taught in St John's Gospel: "He who believes in him is not condemned; he who does not believe is condemned already, because he has not believed in the name of the only Son of God" (*Jn* 3:18).

Dismas, therefore, a condemned man who freely admits his guilt, is acquitted and is promised the reward of eternal life. Thus Jesus said: "As Moses lifted up the serpent in the wilderness, so must the Son of Man be lifted up, that whoever believes in him may have eternal life" (*Jn* 3:14-15). Yes, Jesus is lifted up on the cross so that we may look and see and believe in the limitless love of God for us, and it is through his divine love that we shall be saved for eternal life. We shall be saved because, seeing a perfectly innocent man dying on the cross for us, we shall be moved to love him, to trust him, to call upon him as Lord and God. *Behold him, who takes away the sins of the world.*

Keeping our eyes fixed on Christ who is the truth and the life also enables us, boldly yet humbly, to face up to who we are, to what we have done. Consider the words of the good thief: "We are receiving the due reward of our deeds; but this man has done nothing wrong." What we see here is contrition, sorrow for sin, an act of repentance as the good thief admits his fault. Repentance is the fundamental and necessary condition for receiving the forgiveness and mercy of God. It is a gift from God, a movement of the Holy Spirit in the soul that brings us to repentance, to the honesty of admitting our sins and our guilt as Dismas does. The Holy Spirit is also active in the Sacrament of Confession, opening the treasures of paradise to us, those graces and virtues of Christ that strengthen and empower us for the Christian life. So it is principally through this sacrament that we can come before the Lord, and that we can say, as Dismas does: "Jesus remember me."

For, while I remember my sins and my misdeeds, Jesus remembers *me*. He remembers the dust from which he made me, and so also my human weakness and my mortal frailty. He remembers the breath of life which he breathed into my nostrils, and so also that without him I am nothing. He remembers me, my face, my person whom he saw when he hung on the cross. He remembers me for he has known me from all eternity: formed me, loved me into being. Jesus, seeing me as I am, guilty though I am, dies for me because he loves me. "You did not choose me, but I chose you", said the Lord (*Jn* 15:16). And he does this not because I am lovable, as such, but because God *is* love. God is, therefore, being true to his name when he loves us, and remembers us, and opens the kingdom of heaven to all believers.

One final thought: why is the other thief, traditionally called Gestas, not promised paradise? St Luke says: "One of the criminals who were hanged railed at him, saying, 'Are you not the Christ? Save yourself and us!'" On one level, it looks like Gestas is also calling on Jesus to save him. But the difference between him and Dismas is his attitude of disbelief. There is a hint of mockery and of anger in his words, which could come from unrepentance, or maybe from a sense of entitlement. He seems to be thinking "I don't deserve this; I ought not to suffer like this." We are all prone to this kind of attitude: we feel sorry for ourselves even when the circumstances are of our own making or choosing.

In such cases, one does not call on Jesus with faith and trust and humility as Dismas does, but rather to challenge God to prove himself. Especially in times of difficulty and suffering, have we not wanted to challenge God to prove that he can save us? Prove that he loves us? Indeed, prove that he even exists?

At the start of his ministry, Christ was tempted in the wilderness by the Devil to prove that he is God, to prove that the Father loves him. He resists such faithlessness.

"You shall not put the Lord your God to the test" (*Lk* 4:12), says Jesus. Rather, he calls us, even as we suffer in the wilderness like he did, to remember God's word, for "Man does not live by bread alone but on every word that comes from the mouth of God" (*Mt* 4:4). Therefore, when Dismas turns to him in faith, believing in his work as saviour, Jesus gives Dismas his word: "Today you will be with me in paradise." We, in our turn, are thus encouraged to hear the word of God and to believe, to remember in the Gospels what Christ has said and done for us, and so to have faith in him. As St John says: "These are written that you may believe that Jesus is the Christ, the Son of God, and that believing you may have life in his name" (*Jn* 20:31).

Let us once again end with the prayer that the Angel of Peace taught to the holy children of Fatima:

> *"My God, I believe, I adore, I hope and I love Thee! I ask pardon for those who do not believe, do not adore, do not hope and do not love Thee."*

The third word (see *Jn* 19:26, 27):

To Mary, his mother:
Woman, behold your son.
To John:
Behold your mother.

They say that you cannot choose your family, and this is certainly true if we are speaking of our biological birth and our DNA. We are related by blood to a certain family, born of our mother and father. In the natural order of things, we are born of our parents as sheer gift, for parents also cannot choose the kind of child they have, despite the flawed attempts of contemporary eugenics and boutique surrogacy. A child is not a commodity or product ("of the will of the flesh or of the will of man", as St John put it), and ought to be a gift of God freely and lovingly accepted by husband and wife.

God, therefore, coming into this world as man, was also born of a woman and into a family with an ancestry, as we all are. Christ need not have become man in this way, but he chose it because it is the human way and, therefore, the most fitting way for God to become man and to share our human experience. Thus, "born of woman, born under the

law" (*Ga* 4:4), Jesus shared the bloodline of Mary, and so he was descended from Obed, and Nathan, and Zorobabel, and Boaz and Ruth, and David and Mattathias, and a whole host of other exotic names, as the Gospel of St Luke recounts. And Christ's family tree, like all of ours, was a mix of great and noble people, some colourful characters, and some rogues and sinners, even murderers.

However, because Christ is God, unlike us he could in a unique sense *choose* his mother. God prepared Mary to be the Mother of God; his grace preserved her from the stain of original sin from the moment of her conception, and so Mary remained sinless throughout her life. Mary, in her sinlessness, therefore, lived as God had wanted us all to live from the very beginning, had Adam and Eve not fallen into original sin. But because our first parents abused the freedom God had given them, so now, "in the fullness of time" (*Ga* 4:4), God himself provides the remedy for sin by creating Mary free from sin, and then by being born of Mary, born of this very particular and unique woman. As the Catechism says: "To become the mother of the Saviour, Mary 'was enriched by God with gifts appropriate to such a role'" (*Catechism of the Catholic Church* 490).

However, Mary's role as Mother is completed only now on the cross, when Jesus gives her to the Beloved Disciple, and thus makes her Mother of the Church, mother of all who are baptised, mother of those redeemed by Christ, mother of all who truly live through the grace of Christ, *our* mother.

"Behold your mother," he says; and so he gives Mary to be truly our mother. This is something that only God can do. For just as God gave us our natural, biological mothers, so now, from the cross, Christ-as-God gives us a *supernatural* mother who will care for us and nourish us and raise us up to maturity in the order of grace. So Christ gives to Mary the perfection of her role as the sinless Virgin Mother of the Saviour, which is that she should lead us little Christians to perfection; that she should be our intercessor in our struggle against sin; and that she should be a mediator of those graces we need so that we may grow in holiness, growing "to the measure of the stature of the fullness of Christ" (*Ep* 4:13). Christ's own perfectly created and specially chosen mother is therefore given to become our mother, specially chosen for each of us too. For we too have been chosen by God – chosen, from all eternity, for friendship and a place in paradise with him.

In the *Stabat Mater*, which is sung at this time of year, Mary is addressed as "*Mater, fons amoris*": O Mother, fount of love. As such, Mary our Mother has to teach us Christ-like charity – she shows us how to love as Christ does, and she guides us in the ways of that grace-filled love which embraces suffering and sacrifice. Thus, standing by the cross, she leads us to contemplate the sacrificial love of Jesus. With her heart pierced, she suffers with Christ, and so she teaches us to unite our own sufferings with Jesus's. For just as our own mothers would have taught us to speak, taught us how to live, and shown us love, so Mary as Fount of Love prepares us to speak and act like her beloved son, teaching us how to live as saints now and in the life to come, guiding us in the ways of love as love will inevitably also pierce our own hearts, and showing us how we can be united to her crucified son.

As St Paul says, if I "have not love, I am nothing" (*1 Co* 13:2). Mary, therefore, teaches us to be *something* – to have love and so to become a new creation through grace. It is not surprising that St John, with whom Our Lady lived after Christ's death, became himself a great writer and teacher of divine love. As he wrote in his first epistle: "Beloved, let us love one another; for love is of God, and he who loves is born of God and knows God" (*1 Jn* 4:7). He who loves is born of God. Therefore, through the theological virtue of charity given to us, and through our exercise of this virtue, by works of love, we are re-born of God. Thus, as loving Christians we have God for our father. From the cross, then, Christ ensures that we shall have Mary as our mother showing us by her example how we can better love one another; Mary schools us in charity. Jesus says to the Beloved Disciple "Behold your mother"; he tells us, if we wish to best learn the way of love, to look to Mary, to behold her as our mother.

Looking at Our Blessed Mother, what shall we see? We behold her deep love for Christ: following him all the way to Calvary, she willingly suffers with him. For, all who love will also have to suffer. Like Christ, who, out of the depths of his divine love, suffers greatly for sinful humanity, so too Mary stands by the cross to share in Christ's passion, and with her sinless son she, the Immaculate One, endures suffering for the sins of humanity. St Paul says: "Love bears all things…endures all things" (*1 Co* 13:7). Simeon foretold that a sword would pierce Mary's immaculate heart, for she was a woman full of compassion, full of love. We catch a glimpse of this neighbourly love and care when, at the wedding at Cana, she notices the couple's predicament – they have run out of wine – and, to spare them social embarrassment and shame, goes to Christ and asks him to help them. Let us behold our mother, let us look always to her, the fount of love, meditating on her actions perhaps when we pray the Holy Rosary, learning from her humble example of compassion, service and love.

Let us end with the prayer that the Angel of Peace taught to the holy children of Fatima:

> *"My God, I believe, I adore, I hope and I love Thee! I ask pardon for those who do not believe, do not adore, do not hope and do not love Thee."*

Maundy Thursday

The fourth word (see *Mt* 27:46):

To God, his Father:
My God, my God, why have you forsaken me?

On Palm Sunday last year, my classmate from primary school, whom I have known since I was six but had not seen in over thirty years, was visiting London from Korea, and came to our Solemn Mass that day. The response to the responsorial psalm that day was this, the fourth word of Christ from the cross: "My God, my God, why have you forsaken me?" It is, of course, also the opening lines of Psalm 21, a psalm attributed to King David. After the Mass, as he was waiting for his cab, he said to me: "I have never really understood those words of Jesus. Why did he say, 'My God, my God, why have you forsaken me?'" What answer could I give in the one minute before his cab came?

I told him, briefly, what I will expand upon now: Christ, the Second Person of the Trinity, is, of course, never separated from nor abandoned by the Father. This would be impossible. However, in becoming man and sharing our human condition, God willed and lovingly chose to share our human experience down to the very depths and dark pits of depression that we can experience. On the cross,

Christ endures not only bodily pain but also the sufferings of the soul, psychological pain. Indeed, as St John Henry Newman says: “It was not the body that suffered, but the soul in the body; it was the soul and not the body which was the seat of the suffering of the Eternal Word.” Thus, Jesus says in Gethsemane: “My soul is very sorrowful, even to death” (*Mt* 26:38), and this mental anguish is so great that the Evangelists note that Jesus sweats blood. This is a rare medical condition called hematidrosis, and it is caused by extreme distress or fear, feelings our Lord experienced as he began to undergo his passion for our sake.

On the cross, when the crucified Lord utters these words, he expresses, as “true man” and as the Head of humanity (see *1 Co* 11:3), the fullest extent of the psychological sufferings that human beings can experience. In permitting himself to endure everything that we human beings have to endure, so Christ chooses to share this deepest of existential pains: the sense of being alone, without a loving father, or even a loving God. Indeed, to think that there is no God, to truly be an atheist, creates a deep sadness of soul that can depress and warp a whole society. But even here, in this deep sorrow, a sorrow very much of our times, Christ our God wills to be present. Christ lovingly chooses to suffer this sorrow with us; with atheists; with those who have been abandoned by a parent; with people who do not experience God’s love and closeness; with those who cannot pray and are sorrowful as a result; with those who might, in times of sickness, distress and grief, feel that God is absent; with all who are confounded by the world's terrors and uncertainties and heartaches, and who wonder: "Where is God? Why has he forsaken or abandoned us?"

Jesus, however, is not aloof from this existential angst. He is not distant and uncaring of our anguish. For here on the cross, he cries out and gives voice to the deep sorrow of soul that afflicts so many of our contemporaries, and that perhaps also gnaws at us. But Jesus cries out with these words of Psalm 21, which thus remind us that this feeling of the absence, the forsakenness, of God, is an experience that great religious men, such as David and Job, have all endured. These holy seers of times past have stared into the abyss, confronted the silence, and they all point to this moment of the cross, to Jesus who calls out, giving voice to the deepest sorrow of the human heart: "My God, my God, why have you forsaken me?"

Can you see the profound love and compassion of Christ? He so desires to show us that he is Emmanuel, God-*with*-us, that he wills even to undergo this anguish with us. He is not play-acting, but, in his humanity, freely willing it; Christ really does *feel* as we sometimes feel: abandoned by God. Except that now, even in those depths of depression and angst, we cannot any longer be abandoned by God. Through his crucifixion, Christ is now evermore there with us in our forsakenness. Therefore the psalm (139) rightly says: "O where can I go from your spirit, or where can I flee from your face? If I climb the heavens, you are there. If I lie in the grave, you are there." For "even darkness is not dark for you and the night is as clear as the day". Where, then, is God? Right there, with us, with you, in the darkness!

Cling to these words of the Lord, hold on in your minds to this bitter moment on the cross. Then, in the darkness, in those times when you feel as though you are lying in your grave, remember that Christ too endured this sense of being abandoned by God, and that he lovingly chooses to enter into our darkness in order to make it "as clear as day". For his presence is the light; he is God-with-us.

Let us end with the prayer that the Angel of Peace taught to the holy children of Fatima:

> *"My God, I believe, I adore, I hope and I love Thee! I ask pardon for those who do not believe, do not adore, do not hope and do not love Thee."*

Good Friday

The fifth word (see *Jn 19:28*):

To all: *I thirst.*

When I hear these words of Christ, I always think of St Teresa of Kolkata and her Missionaries of Charity. In each of their convent chapels there will be a crucifix behind the altar, and next to the crucifix, these words, the fifth word of the dying Lord Jesus, will have been marked out on the wall: "I thirst".

Traditionally, the scriptures and the Saints have spoken about the thirst of the human soul for God. Psalm 63, for example, says: "O God you are my God, for you I long, for you my soul is thirsting like a dry weary land without water" (*Ps* 63:1), and St Augustine famously wrote in his spiritual autobiography that "our hearts are restless until they rest in God". When I was a teenager, and as I was thinking about becoming a Catholic, both these sentences meant a lot to me. They seemed to speak about my deepest longing for God, my desire to know and experience the love of God, and so I became an inquirer, then a catechumen, and was baptised a Catholic, aged sixteen.

However, even before we can speak of our love, our longings and our desire for God, we must ponder and

behold first of all the unfathomable love of God for man: a love that takes him to this day, Good Friday; a love that leads Christ to willingly suffer and be nailed to the cross. St John the Beloved Disciple said: "In this is love, not that we loved God but that he loved us and sent his Son to be the expiation for our sins" (*1 Jn* 4:10). In going up to the cross, Christ is leading humanity as a shepherd leads his flock, through the "valley of the shadow of death", and guiding us to the green pastures of paradise (see *Ps* 22), where he will satisfy the deepest thirst of the human soul: our longing for God, for happiness, for divine love. Jesus promises that "whoever drinks of the water that I shall give him will never thirst; the water that I shall give him will become in him a spring of water welling up to eternal life" (*Jn* 4:14). So, yes, we *can* satisfy the thirst, the restlessness, the angst that we experience if we draw near to Christ; rejecting all that dehydrates us, we can "draw water from the wells of salvation" (see *Is* 12:3).

But drawing close to Christ – going to him and choosing to be with him – not only satisfies our thirst for love, but, more astoundingly, it also satisfies God's longing for us, for *our* love. This is how the Saints have understood the thirst of Christ on the cross. As Mother Teresa said in one of her letters to her sisters:

> At this most difficult time He proclaimed, "I thirst." And people thought He was thirsty in an ordinary way, and

> they gave Him vinegar straight away; but it was not for that which he thirsted – it was for our love, our affection; that intimate attachment to Him, and that sharing of His passion. He used, 'I thirst' instead of 'Give Me your love'… 'I thirst.' Let us hear Him saying it to me and saying it to you.

In every generation, Christ has given us saints to remind us of his thirst for our love, attention and gratitude. To this day, the Lord continues to wait for us to show him our love; he waits for us especially in the Eucharist, in the tabernacle.

In June 1675, Jesus revealed his Sacred Heart to St Margaret Mary Alacoque and said to her:

> Behold the Heart which has so loved men that it has spared nothing, even to exhausting and consuming Itself, in order to testify Its love; and in return, I receive from the greater part only ingratitude, by their irreverence and sacrilege, and by the coldness and contempt they have for Me in the Eucharist. But what I feel most keenly is that it is hearts which are consecrated to Me that treat Me thus.

Hence, it is vital that we who are priests and religious should renew our love for the Eucharist, especially by adoring the Lord in the tabernacle and celebrating Mass with reverence, care and attention. And to all of us, the Lord asks: Will we not come and spend some time with him? Will we not come to church and adore him, love him, speak to him who is exposed on our altar day after day?

Only on this day, Good Friday, of all the days in the year, is the Blessed Sacrament not waiting in the tabernacle of our churches. On this day, the day when we commemorate the Lord's death, the tabernacle is emptied, and our churches feel somehow devoid of life, emptied of the Presence, museum-like rather than a holy place for a real encounter with the living God. When we come into church without any regard or reverence for the holy and living God who dwells in the tabernacle, we turn this church building into just an empty shell or mere pitiful museum of our fragile memories. Without the Blessed Sacrament, without God, our life becomes emptied of all genuine meaning, and we fade away as a civilisation, as a community, as human beings.

Hence, the psalmist said: "You hide your face, they are dismayed" (*Ps* 104:29). On this day, Good Friday, the Blessed Sacrament is hidden away from us, and our tabernacles stand empty as a reminder that this greatest of gifts is not to be taken for granted. Rather, he is here for us, to lead us through the "valley of the shadow of death", to be "the way, the truth and the life for us", leading us to eternal life. He longs to love us and to help us: he thirsts for us to come to him and to love him, to realise our deep need of him, and so to desire and long for him.

For that is how we are made. As St Augustine said: "You have made us for yourself, and our hearts are restless, until they can find rest in you." Therefore, from the tabernacle, in the Holy Eucharist, Christ calls out to us again and again: "Come to me, all who labour and are heavy laden, and I will give you rest. Take my yoke upon you, and learn from me; for I am gentle and lowly in heart, and you will find rest for your souls" (*Mt* 11:28-29). Daily, the Lord invites us to rest in him. At least once a week, on Sunday, he invites us to be at rest by coming to Holy Mass and giving that time and our attention, as far as is humanly possible, to him.

Christ thirsts for the chance to satisfy the deepest hunger of the human heart. He thirsts to give himself to you in the Eucharist. He thirsts for you to come to him and to let him love you.

Hence Mother Teresa wrote:

> Jesus wants me to tell you again, especially in this Holy Week, how much love He has for each one of you – beyond all you can imagine. I worry some of you still have not really met Jesus – one to one – you and Jesus alone. We may spend time in chapel – but have you seen with the eyes of your soul how He looks at you with love? Do you really know the living Jesus – not from books but from being with Him in your heart? Have you heard the loving words He speaks to you? Ask for the grace, He is longing to give it. Until you can hear Jesus

in the silence of your own heart, you will not be able to hear Him saying "I thirst" in the hearts of the poor…

Be careful of all that can block that personal contact with the living Jesus. The Devil may try to use the hurts of life, and sometimes our own mistakes – to make you feel it is impossible that Jesus really loves you, is really cleaving to you. This is a danger for all of us. And so sad, because it is completely opposite of what Jesus is really wanting, waiting to tell you. Not only that He loves you, but even more – He longs for you. He misses you when you don't come close. He thirsts for you. He loves you always, even when you don't feel worthy. When not accepted by others, even by yourself sometimes – He is the one who always accepts you. My children, you don't have to be different for Jesus to love you. Only believe – You are precious to Him. Bring all you are suffering to His feet – only open your heart to be loved by Him as you are.

Let us end with the prayer that the Angel of Peace taught to the holy children of Fatima:

"My God, I believe, I adore, I hope and I love Thee! I ask pardon for those who do not believe, do not adore, do not hope and do not love Thee."

Holy Saturday

The sixth and seventh words (see *Jn* 19:30; *Lk* 23:46):

To the world:
It is finished.
And to God:
Father, into your hands I commend my spirit.

For this final day, I have combined the sixth and seventh words of Jesus on the cross: St John records "It is finished" as the final words of the Lord, whereas St Luke has this line from Psalm 31 as Jesus's final words: "Father, into your hands, I commend my spirit." But the Gospels agree that after his final utterance, Jesus "yielded up his spirit" (*Mt* 27:50; *Jn* 19:30), that is to say, his breath. So, as the psalm cited by St Luke put it, Jesus commends his spirit, his last breath, to the Father.

Anyone who has been by the bedside of a dying person will know that the sound of a person's breathing is often the most important indication of their struggle for life. Sitting there, we watch the breathing and, more importantly, we listen to it becoming more ragged, more laboured, more faint. It is as if life fades away or is breathed out, just as, at our creation, the Spirit of God – the breath of life – was breathed into us so that we are alive. At death we become

fundamentally breathless. For all living creatures, therefore, breath is synonymous with life, and the Latin word *spiritus* (or the Greek *pneuma*), which is used by St Luke here, essentially means breath. So, when Jesus is said to yield up his spirit, or to commend his spirit to the Father, it means he gives his breath, his life, into God's care.

However, because of the uniqueness of Christ's person, being both God and man, Jesus's human death differs from ours in one crucial respect: whereas we *lose* our life, dying either passively or unwillingly, Christ *chooses* the moment of his death, when all is thus accomplished. So, the word recorded by St John, "It is finished", is indicative: there is a sense of a mission accomplished, a purposeful act completed. Christ's death is not without meaning but is willed for a reason that accords with God's love for fallen humanity. So, in obedience to the Father, Christ lovingly wills to undergo the agony of the cross; he chooses to suffer on the cross, both in body and soul, all that we as human beings can suffer; and he actively wills to die in union with all men and women of all ages, sharing fully in the extremities of our natural human condition. At no point is Christ's will disengaged or passive in this saving work of the passion and cross. Why? Because God *loves* you and me, and his love is all-consuming, fully engaged and ever attentive.

St John Henry Newman reflects as follows:

> He took a body in order that He might suffer; He became man, that He might suffer as man; and when His hour was come, that hour of Satan and of darkness, the hour when sin was to pour its full malignity upon Him, it followed that He offered Himself wholly, a holocaust, a whole burnt-offering; – as the whole of His body, stretched out upon the Cross, so the whole of His soul, His whole advertence [meaning *attention*], His whole consciousness, a mind awake, a sense acute, a living co-operation, a present, absolute intention, not a virtual permission, not a heartless submission, – this did He present to His tormentors. His passion was an action; He lived most energetically, while He lay languishing, fainting, and dying. Nor did He die, except by an act of the will; for He bowed His head, in command as well as in resignation, and said, "Father, into Thy hands I commend My Spirit;" He gave the word, He surrendered His soul, He did not lose it.

Christ gave the word, "It is finished", and with his final speech, he commended his life to the Father, breathing forth his spirit at last. The beauty of this word *spiritus*, or *pneuma*, is that it immediately calls to mind the Third Person of the Blessed Trinity, the Holy Spirit of God who, as God's Breath, is the 'Giver of Life', as we say in the Creed. Christ, therefore, by his dying on the cross, finishes the work of our redemption from sin and suffering and death, offering his all as a holocaust to the Father. Fittingly, Jesus yields his spirit, as, in his dying, he both lovingly offers his life to the Father and gives to the world the promised Spirit of God who is the giver of life and love itself. And so, by dying, Christ gives us life, and he awakens love in the soul. St John of the Cross thus calls out to the Holy Spirit as the "south wind…you that waken love" and says:

> And in your sweet breathing,
> Filled with good and glory
> How tenderly you swell my heart with love.

Life is intimately related to love. Herbert McCabe, O.P., said: "If you do not love, you will not be alive." But the paradox is that loving well, loving effectively, takes us to the cross; it unites us to Jesus who dies for love of mankind. Hence McCabe also said: "If you love effectively, you will be killed."

What, then, are we to do with this life that has been given to us? If we fear death, and fear pain, and fear all that there is to fear in the world, such that we do not dare to love any but ourselves, then will we ever truly live? C.S. Lewis rightly observes that:

> To love at all is to be vulnerable. Love anything, and your heart will certainly be wrung and possibly be broken. If you want to make sure of keeping it intact, you must give your heart to no one, not even to an

> animal. Wrap it carefully round with hobbies and little luxuries; avoid all entanglements; lock it up safe in the casket or coffin of your selfishness. But in that casket – safe, dark, motionless, airless – it will change. It will not be broken; it will become unbreakable, impenetrable, irredeemable. The alternative to tragedy, or at least to the risk of tragedy, is damnation. The only place outside Heaven where you can be perfectly safe from all the dangers and perturbations of love is Hell.

Therefore, we must love, for to live *is* to love, and to have lived fully is to have loved selflessly, even to the point of sacrifice, just as Jesus and Mary show us. The Holy Spirit, we pray, will swell our hearts with love, so that we shall be healed of the wounds of sin; we shall be made whole again; and we shall be made ready for eternal life. As Jesus says: "Unless a grain of wheat falls into the earth and dies, it remains alone; but if it dies, it bears much fruit. He who loves his life loses it, and he who hates his life in this world will keep it for eternal life" (*Jn* 12:24-25).

It seems that the goal of this life, given to us from God, is that we should follow Christ in offering up our life and all that we do to God the Father, in love. Each of us is being trained and taught in this life, with all its sorrows and difficulties and uncertainties, ultimately, to commend our spirit to the Father, to lovingly hand ourselves over to him when all seems finished for us. Thus C.S. Lewis says:

> We shall draw nearer to God, not by trying to avoid the sufferings inherent in all loves, but by accepting them and offering them to Him; throwing away all defensive armour. If our hearts need to be broken, and if He chooses this as the way in which they should break, so be it.

Christ's Sacred Heart is pierced with a lance, his blessed Mother's immaculate heart is pierced with a sword, both hearts are broken by love. So will it be for us if we dare to love; if we continue on this mad adventure that we call Christian discipleship; if we choose daily to deny ourselves, pick up our cross, and follow Jesus to Calvary and beyond (see *Mt* 16:24). For if we do not love, then we are already dead. But if we do, if we commit our lives into the Father's hand, trusting in his providence and love, his mercy and good promises, then, as Julian of Norwich saw in her visions of divine love, "all shall be well, and all manner of thing shall be well."

Although our hearts may have been broken, remember these words of the Lord to us. They are a covenant of love in which God binds himself closely to us. They are a bond that has been ratified on the cross and that is renewed in every Mass. God has promised: "A new heart I will give you, and a new spirit I will put within you; and I will take out of your flesh the heart of stone and give you a heart of flesh. And I will put my spirit within you…and you shall be my people, and I will be your God" (see *Ezk* 36:26-28). If we are so intimately united to God, truly of one heart and mind with Christ, then death and suffering have less power over us, for death gives way to life, and our darknesses shall become as bright as day.

Therefore, at the mother of all vigils tonight, the whole Church will proclaim in the Exsultet:

This is the night
that even now, throughout the world,
sets Christian believers apart from worldly vices
and from the gloom of sin,
leading them to grace
and joining them to his holy ones.

This is the night, when Christ broke the
prison-bars of death
and rose victorious from the underworld.
Our birth would have been no gain,
had we not been redeemed.
O wonder of your humble care for us!
O love, O charity beyond all telling,
to ransom a slave you gave away your Son!

O truly necessary sin of Adam,
destroyed completely by the Death of Christ!

O happy fault
that earned for us so great, so glorious a Redeemer!

Let us end with the prayer that the Angel of Peace taught to the holy children of Fatima:

> *"My God, I believe, I adore, I hope and I love Thee! I ask pardon for those who do not believe, do not adore, do not hope and do not love Thee."*